Healthy food

Photography by Bill Thomas

We all need to eat food.

We need to drink
lots of water
every day, too.

Food helps children to grow, play,
and do their school work.

Some foods are very good for us.

bread

pasta

cereals

rice

We can eat these foods every day.

Vegetables are very good for us.
We can eat them every day.

Some vegetables are green
and some are red.

Some vegetables are white
and some are orange.

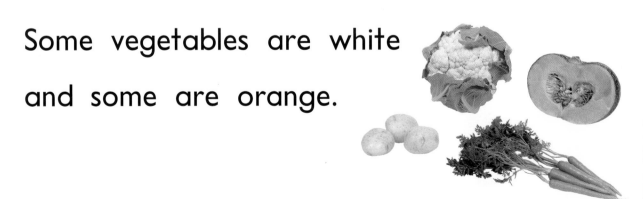

We can eat fruit
every day.

Apples, oranges
and bananas are fruit.

Fruit is very good for us.

Children need
to drink milk every day.
Milk helps children grow.

Yogurt is made
from milk.

Fish is good for everyone.

We need to eat
some fish, some meat,
or some white beans every day.
We need to eat
some eggs or some cheese, too.

These foods help children to grow.

FISH FILLETS

TROUT

COD

We must not eat

a lot of **these** foods.

cakes

cookies

fries

candy

But it is fun to eat them sometimes.

Eat little

Eat some

Eat lots

Don't forget to drink water every day!